# LITERARY PORTSMOUTH

Steve Wallis

AMBERLEY

First published 2013

Amberley Publishing
The Hill, Stroud, Gloucestershire, GL5 4EP
www.amberley-books.com

Copyright © Steve Wallis, 2013

The right of Steve Wallis to be identified as the
Author of this work has been asserted in accordance
with the Copyrights, Designs and Patents Act 1988.

ISBN  978 1 4456 1646 9 (print)
ISBN  978 1 4456 1665 0 (ebook)

British Library Cataloguing in Publication Data.
A catalogue record for this book is available from the
British Library.

Typesetting by Amberley Publishing.
Printed in Great Britain.

# Contents

# Acknowledgements

I would like very much to thank Portsmouth Historic Dockyard, especially Holly Westwood, the Press Officer; Father Roger Calder of the parish church of St Alban, Copnor; Portsmouth City Council, especially Rosalinda Hardiman, Joe McGoldrick, Rachel McMinn and Jane Mee; Emily Preston and Glyn Williams for their assistance in the production of this book.

I have referred to a number of books and websites while writing this book. The main books are listed in the bibliography, and there are three particularly valuable websites that I would like to mention here: the 'Portsmouth Literature Map' on Google Maps, the University of Portsmouth's 'Dickens and the Victorian City – Portsmouth Map' and the website of The Nevil Shute Foundation.

# Introduction

Mention the literary associations of Portsmouth to people from outside the area and you may well get a response along the lines of, 'Oh yes, Charles Dickens was born there, wasn't he?' Indeed he was, but many more literary figures have associations with the city; Sherlock Holmes was first written about in Portsmouth, and the mid-twentieth century's most popular thriller writer ran a major business in the city. In this book, I have aimed to illustrate this greater depth of the city's literary connections, looking at the wide variety of writers who have lived in, worked in and often written about the place.

I have concentrated more on the historical figures, but have included some living writers to show that writing in Portsmouth is not just something that happened in the past, but is alive and well today. I have also chosen several individuals who have particularly strong connections and interesting stories to tell, and have looked at them in more detail.

I must emphasise, though, that this is just a selection. The reader may well know of others, and the fact that a particular writer is not included or not looked at in detail is not intended to denigrate them in any way. Rather, it shows just how extensive the city's role in literature has been, how much there is to discover about the place, and above all how enjoyable it is to find out more.

In choosing my subjects, I have followed the expansion of the city. The Portsmouth of a few hundred years ago was, of course, a much smaller place clustered by the harbour, and here was where contemporary literary activity was based. By the later eighteenth century, there was considerable expansion inland, and this is reflected in locations associated with literary figures from then onwards – Charles Dickens' birthplace is over half a mile inland from the old walls, and by the twentieth century, the urban area was effectively filling Portsea Island. To reflect this, I have taken as my subject area the wider Portsmouth conurbation, including places like Portchester and Gosport, although I have strayed beyond this once or twice to look at particular places with significant links to the literary history of the place.

This leads me on to the subject of place names. Locations such as Southsea and Fratton are today seen as areas or suburbs of the city, but they were once

The city skyline seen from Portsdown Hill. The Spinnaker Tower is prominent on the right.

distinct places in their own right (the latter being a village originally called Froddington, for example) before being enveloped by urban expansion. Furthermore, it now seems natural to refer to Portsmouth as a city, but it only became one in 1926. Before then it was technically a borough, although people probably thought of it more as a town.

In researching this book, I have come to appreciate just what a diverse and fascinating place Portsmouth is. There is much variety in its buildings, landscape and people, and I was often surprised as I walked around it, for example finding

A view of Old Portsmouth from the Gosport side of Portsmouth Harbour. The tower of the cathedral is towards the left, and Tower House and the Round Tower are on the right.

a row of lovely Georgian buildings that had survived the bombing of the Second World War and is now hidden away in an area of modern development. The sea, of course, adds greatly to Portsmouth's character, as does the varied coastline with the great inlets of Portsmouth and Langstone Harbours. Portsdown Hill also adds a great deal to the locality – it is not just somewhere to go to enjoy views of the city, but also forms a boundary with the rest of England, marking out Portsmouth as somewhere special.

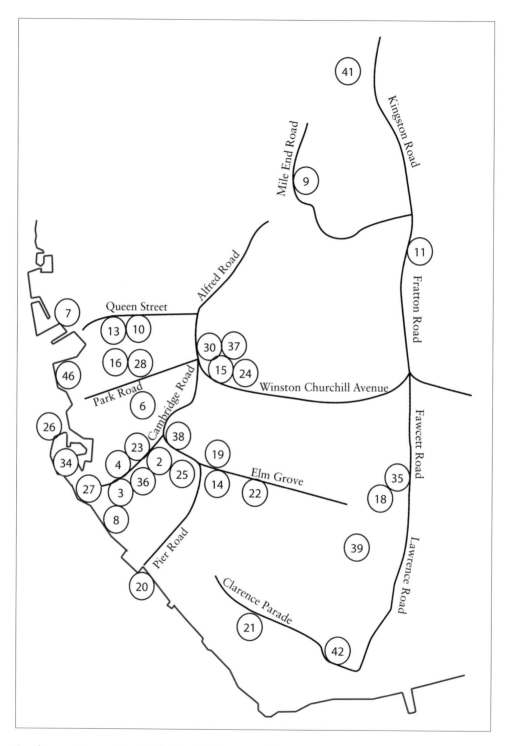

South-west Portsea Island including Old Portsmouth.

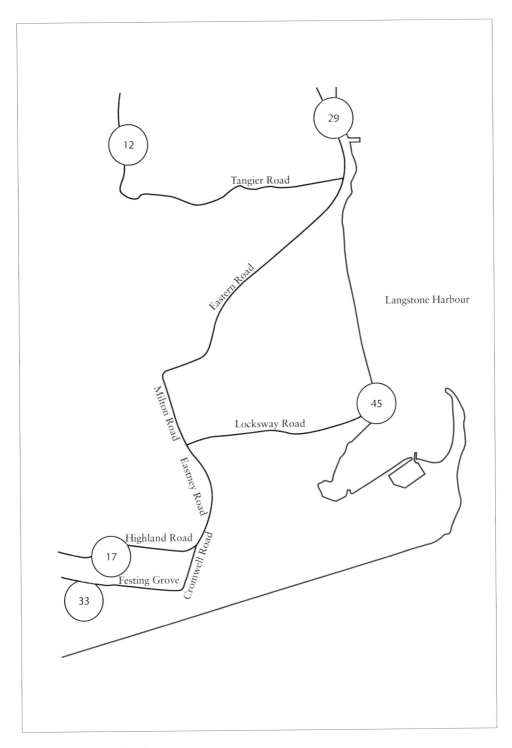

South-east Portsea Island.

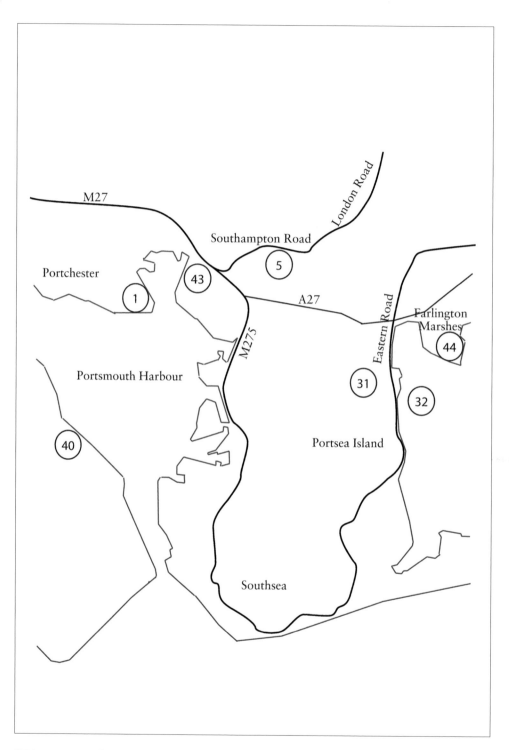

Wider Portsmouth conurbation.

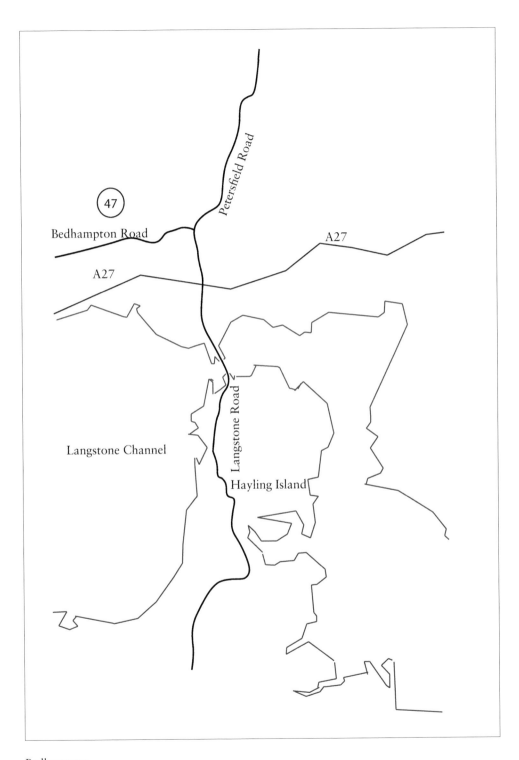

Bedhampton.

# Key

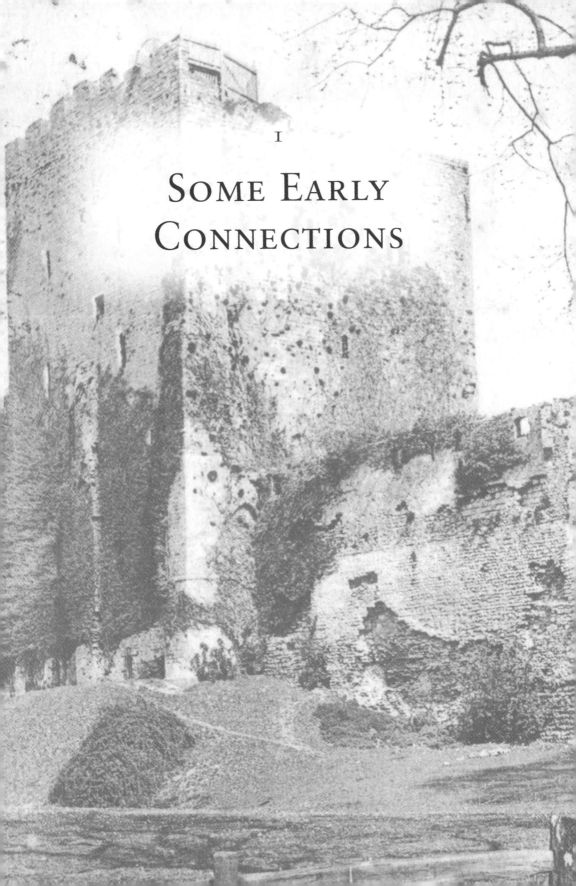

# I

# SOME EARLY
# CONNECTIONS

An aerial view of Portchester Castle, near the mouth of Portsmouth Harbour. The medieval castle, probably dating from the eleventh century, sits in one corner of a late Roman fort. The site is now in the care of English Heritage.

## William Shakespeare (1564–1616)

One of the earliest literary references to the Portsmouth area is found in Shakespeare's play *Henry V*, albeit obliquely. That King's expedition to France in 1415 that culminated in the great victory at the Battle of Agincourt began with a mustering of troops at Portsmouth, Southampton and Winchester, and it was during this time that a plot involving the Earl of Cambridge to assassinate the King in Southampton was discovered. The Earl and two others were executed, and the King sailed for France from Portchester Castle. The incident is an important element in the early part of Shakespeare's play, although no local names are mentioned specifically.

Two views of Portchester Castle, the older dating from *c.* 1900. In the old view there is a mound in front of the tower. Presumably this was part of the moat system. It does not survive today.

The defensive walls of old Portsmouth that Pepys admired and enjoyed, as people do today.

### Samuel Pepys (1633–1703)

On 1 May 1661, the famous diarist, Samuel Pepys, and his wife arrived by coach in Portsmouth. He had recently been appointed Clerk of the King's Ships and this was his first visit to the port where so many of them were based. He stayed at an inn called the Red Lion, but Pepys was not impressed by the accommodation there, although he was rather flattered when several officers from the dockyard visited him. While here, he walked around Portsmouth's defences and noted in his diary that it seemed 'a very pleasant and strong place'. He also visited the house in the High Street, where the unpopular George Villiers, Duke of Buckingham, had been murdered by an army officer in 1628. This property now bears the name Buckingham House to commemorate the killing.

Buckingham House in the High Street, which had only recently been converted from an inn into a private residence at the time of the Duke's assassination.

William Cobbett (1763–1835)
Cobbett was born in Farnham in Surrey. He was a farmer and journalist, the latter linking with his campaigning against corruption in government and public affairs. Today, however, he is best known for his *Rural Rides*, a series of journeys he made through southern England and the Midlands that were published in the 1820s. Together they make for fascinating reading as social history.

Long before this, probably in 1783, he came to Portsmouth in an attempt to join the Navy. However, once onboard a man-o'-war called the *Pegasus*, he was dissuaded from joining by the captain. This man, whose name was Berkeley, told him of the harsh punishments inflicted in the Navy, as well as the general unpleasantness of the rest of the seafaring life, and then kindly took Cobbett back to shore.

Cobbett instead decided to join the Army, and spent the period between 1785 and 1791 in Canada with the 54th (West Norfolk) Regiment. He returned with it to Portsmouth on 3 November 1791 and obtained his discharge from the Army the following month.

### Susanna Rowson (1762–1824)

Susanna Rowson is the first of a number of persons in this book who were born in Portsmouth, but who moved away in childhood to achieve fame elsewhere. She was born Susanna Haswell in Penny Street and soon after, like most children in the area, she was baptised at St Thomas' church. Her father was a lieutenant in the Navy, and he took her to Massachusetts when she was only five years old. They became prisoners during the American War of

Penny Street, where Susanna Haswell was born, runs parallel to the High Street on its south-east side. Although there have been changes resulting from wartime bombing and redevelopment, many of the buildings that were here when Susanna was born survive today.

Two views of the parish church of St Thomas, where Susanna Haswell was baptised. The old view dates from *c.* 1910. Parts of the church date from the twelfth century and it became a cathedral in 1927, the year after Portsmouth was granted city status.

St Thomas' new status as a cathedral was reflected in the addition of a substantial western extension during the 1930s. Here we see that extension from the same side of the building as that from which the previous views were taken. Also, on the left there is the tower, which was rebuilt in the late seventeenth century together with other parts of the church, which were damaged during the Civil War.

Independence, went to Canada through a prisoner exchange, and finally got back to England. Susanna became an actress, poet and writer, and married a William Rowson. Undoubtedly, her most famous claim to fame is that her *Charlotte Temple* was the bestselling novel in the United States for over fifty years from its publication in 1791.

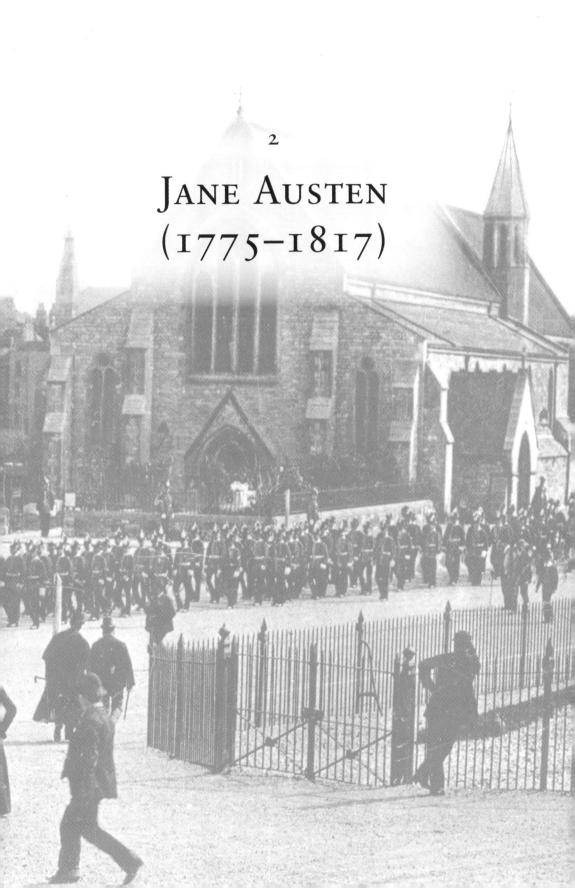

2

# JANE AUSTEN
# (1775–1817)

Jane Austen is now seen as one of this country's greatest female writers, and her novels are regularly adapted for television and film. Nevertheless, in her own lifetime her works were not recognised to any great degree, and it was some fifty years after her death before they gained any degree of popularity.

Her father George was rector at Steventon in Hampshire, and Jane was the second youngest of eight children. Six of her siblings were boys. In 1800, George retired from the ministry and moved the family to Bath, where he died the following year. In 1809, Jane and her mother and sister moved back to Hampshire, to a house at Chawton that belonged to her brother Edward. She lived here for the rest of her life, and it was during this period that her great novels were published.

The third of these was *Mansfield Park*, published in 1814. Jane had visited Portsmouth on a number of occasions, particularly to visit her brothers Francis and Charles, who were stationed here while in the Navy, and she sets some of this novel in the town, on several occasions referring to places with which she was clearly familiar.

Jane Austen's elder brother, who rose to be Admiral Sir Francis Austen, is buried at Wymering's parish church of St Peter and St Paul. Wymering is now a suburb of Portsmouth on the lower slopes of Portsdown Hill.

The novel was written when Austen was in her thirties and so, by the standards of the time, a confirmed spinster. It is highly regarded as social satire, and most of the characters are a bunch of ne'er-do-wells who are not particularly likeable, which is just what a good satire needs. As well as the Portsmouth setting, Austen put other elements of her family background into the story.

The heroine is Fanny Price, who one authority says 'is both stoical and a wet blanket'. Fanny's mother, unlike her own sisters, had married badly, to a Lieutenant of Marines based in Portsmouth. He became disabled from duty, but continued to spend the same amount on drink, while his wife continued to produce children. After some pleading, Fanny, who is the eldest daughter, is sent at the age of ten to live with the family of her wealthy maternal uncle, Sir Thomas Bertram, at Mansfield Park in Northamptonshire, making for one less child for her mother to feed and clothe.

She then spends the majority of the novel growing up at Mansfield Park, but towards the end is sent back to Portsmouth because it is thought that she is getting too close to Sir Thomas' son Edmund. The final chapters describe what happens to Fanny in Portsmouth, and there are several references to real locations.

As Fanny comes into Portsmouth, she goes across a drawbridge over a moat. This must be a reference to going through Landport Gate, which once brought Landport Road in through the military defences of Old Portsmouth, and still can be seen today beside St George's Road. Around the same time, she wonders at all the new houses that are being built, which sounds like Austen's own impression upon seeing new building within the old town and expansion outside the defences on her visits to her brothers.

Fanny then finds her family, who are living in not particularly pleasant conditions in a narrow side street off the High Street. We find such streets nowadays, although they no longer show signs of poverty.

After the society she mingled with at Mansfield Park, Fanny is rather snobbish with the locals and does not think highly of the Portsmouth 'social set'. However, things improve when Henry Crawford, one of the characters from Northamptonshire, pays a visit. Fanny's father gives Henry and Fanny a tour of the naval dockyard, and Henry and the Prices attend a Sunday service at the Garrison chapel.

Two views of the Landport Gate. The gate was rebuilt in 1760 out of Portland stone. The rest of Portsmouth's defences hereabouts were demolished in 1875, leaving the gate as something of an historic island in the modern city.

*This and next page, above:* Examples of housing built around Jane Austen's time in the High Street, Norfolk Street and Old Commercial Road.

*Below:* Peacock Lane, a relatively unchanged side street off the High Street.

*This and next page:* A selection of the dockyard buildings that the fictitious Mr Price would have shown to his daughter and their visitor, and which the real Austen brothers and their sister would have known: (*above*) The Porter's Lodge, built 1708 (*next page, above*) Storehouse No. 11 in 1763 (*next page, below*) Storehouse No. 9 in 1782.

Two contrasting views of the Garrison chapel: the older one was taken *c.*1900, and shows a military parade passing in front of the chapel. The building had been a hospital during the Middle Ages and its roof was destroyed by a German air raid in 1941.

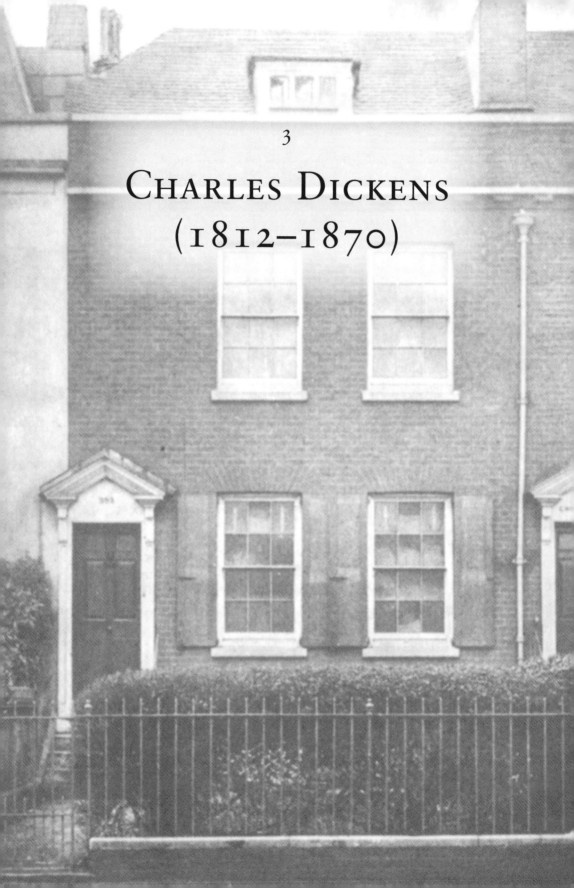

3

# CHARLES DICKENS
# (1812–1870)

Charles Dickens's parents, John Dickens and Elizabeth Burrow, married in the summer of 1809. John was the model for Mr Micawber in his son's novel *David Copperfield*, while Elizabeth may have been the model for Mrs Nickleby in *Nicholas Nickleby*. John had been posted from London to work in the Naval Pay Office at Portsmouth Dockyard, and the dates suggest that he would have met, and perhaps paid, Jane Austen's brothers Francis and Charles. He was introduced to his future wife by her brother Thomas, who also worked in the pay office.

The couple rented a house in what were then the new suburbs of Portsmouth, at No. 1 Mile End Terrace in what is now called Old Commercial Road. They paid £35 per year for the place, an exorbitant amount by normal standards at the time, but the Napoleonic Wars were in progress and many naval officers and other associated personnel needed accommodation in Portsmouth.

Their first child, a daughter called Frances, usually shortened to 'Fanny' as was the current fashion, was born at the house in 1810. Charles was also born here on 7 February 1812.

In June of that year, the Dickens family moved to No. 16 Hawke Street. The reason does not seem to be known, although it was a lot closer to John's place of work and perhaps it was cheaper to rent. This property does not survive.

While at Hawke Street, Elizabeth's sister Mary came to live with them, and this may explain their next move in December 1813 to a larger property out towards Southsea at 38 Wish Street. Again, the house does not survive, but it can be seen as a green space in Kings Road. Although he left the place before his third birthday, Charles was later able to recall details of the house in Wish Street, including the small front garden. A brother, Alfred Allen, was born in March 1814 at this address in Wish Street, but died six months later.

The reason for the family's next move in January 1815 is known. John's posting, which had been temporary and required to deal with the large numbers of naval personnel at Portsmouth, was over and the family moved back to London.

Dickens' associations with the town did not end there, though. For instance, he came to Portsmouth in 1838 while working on *Nicholas Nickleby* and visited the Theatre Royal. He subsequently used details of that theatre in the novel.

One of the ways in which novels were publicised in the nineteenth century was for authors to go on tour, giving public readings of excerpts from their works. Dickens did so regularly, including making trips to the United States. He came to Portsmouth twice for this purpose, giving public readings in November 1858 and May 1866 at the same venue, St George's Hall in St George's Square.

There is one final Portsmouth connection for Dickens in the couch upon which he died. Following his death, this was donated to the Dickens Birthplace Museum by his sister-in-law, Georgina. The death actually occurred at Dickens' home of Gads Hill Place near Higham in Kent, and the museum records two different versions of that event. In the first, he was taken ill on the evening of 8 June 1870 at home, and to avoid distressing him by carrying him up to bed, the family laid him on this couch downstairs, where he died the next day. In the other, he was taken ill on same evening while visiting his mistress, Ellen Ternan, in Peckham. She then hired a carriage to take him back to Gads Hill Place, where again he was laid on this downstairs couch. 'You pays your money, and you takes your choice!'

I would recommend a visit to Highland Road Cemetery in Southsea to all Dickens aficionados. It was opened in 1854 and extended about a quarter of a century later. The information board contains a great deal of information about persons of historic interest who are buried here, including the locations of the graves of a number of persons associated with Dickens, including the family of William Pearce, the landlord of No. 1 Mile End Terrace, Georgina Hayman, who was the model for *Little Dorrit*, and Sir William Dupree, who was instrumental in the birthplace becoming a museum. Intriguingly, and by complete coincidence, since neither originally lived in the area, Dickens' first love, Maria Beadnell, and the last, his mistress Ellen Ternan, are also buried here.

The Naval Pay Office where John Dickens worked.

There is perhaps no better illustration of the wartime setting of Dickens' birth than HMS *Victory*, moored in Portsmouth Historic Dockyard. She was launched in 1765 and was Nelson's flagship at the Battle of Trafalgar in 1805.

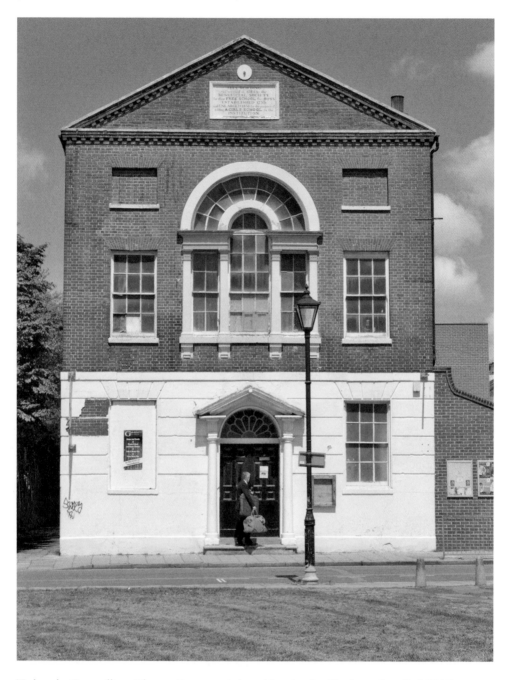

Today, the Groundlings Theatre Company is based in what is affectionately called Old Benny, at No. 42 Kent Street. Its full name is The Old Beneficial Hall, and it was built in 1784. The story goes that Elizabeth Dickens went into labour when pregnant with Charles while attending a dance in this building. This has been disputed, however, because there is no record of a ball that evening. The story could be apocryphal, or perhaps the incident occurred when one of Dickens' siblings was born and the details became confused in family legend.

*This and the next page:* Two Edwardian and one present-day view of the Dickens Birthplace Museum. The property was bought by Portsmouth Corporation in 1903 at the instigation of the mayor, Sir William Thomas Dupree. Presumably it was that body that put the lettering on the eaves, so the picture without them may pre-date the purchase.

The house next door to No.1 Mile End Terrace was the home of William Pearce, who was the Dickens family's landlord.

A wider view of the birthplace in Old Commercial Road. The trees were planted in 1978 as a gift of the Worldwide Dickens Fellowship.

The parish church of St Mary, Kingston, the medieval church in which Dickens was baptised, was rebuilt twice later in the nineteenth century. The old picture was taken around 1900. The first of the pictures shows the church from the same viewpoint – not only have the trees grown to obscure the church, but the tombstones have been removed. The other photograph shows a rather better angle.

*This and next page:* The parish church of St Alban is in Copnor, in Portsmouth's northern suburbs. When it was consecrated in 1914, it was presented with the fifteenth-century font from the church of St Mary, in which not only Charles Dickens but also Isambard Kingdom Brunel were baptised. His Christian faith was always important to Dickens, and he wrote a life of Jesus for his own children.

Hawke Street, the site of Charles Dickens' second home.

The site of No.38 Wish Street, in Kings Road.

The New Theatre Royal was constructed in 1854 on the site of the theatre that Charles Dickens visited sixteen years previously. In turn, it was extensively rebuilt in 1884 and 1900.

Millgate House flats now occupy the site of St George's Hall in St George's Square.

*This and next page:* I found it fascinating to see how Charles Dickens crops up all over Portsmouth. Here are some examples of buildings named after some of his novels that I noticed while preparing this book. Nickleby House and Dombey Court can be found near Dickens' birthplace, while the ornately-decorated Pickwick House is just off St George's Square.

4

# TWO UNHAPPY CHILDHOOD EXPERIENCES

In this chapter, we will look at two famous writers who were born in consecutive years and who both spent part of their childhood in Portsmouth. They came under very different circumstances, but each had an unpleasant time.

Rudyard Kipling

Rudyard Kipling (1865–1936) was a writer and poet strongly linked with the British Empire, about which he cared a great deal. He is best known for his writing today, in works such as *The Jungle Book* and the *Just So Stories*. His short story, 'The Man Who Would Be King', is now particularly well known through the 1975 film starring Sean Connery and Michael Caine.

His father, Lockwood Kipling, accompanied by his wife Alice, had gone out to India to teach at the School of Art and Industry in Bombay. Alice came back to England in 1868 for the birth of her daughter of the same name, and brought young Rudyard with her. The boy's tantrums and general bad behaviour when staying with relatives during this visit may have been the reason why, when the whole family again came back from India in early 1871, they went into lodgings. They stayed at Lorne Lodge in Southsea's Campbell Road, with the Holloway family.

After six months, the parents returned to India, leaving the children in the care of the Holloways. By today's standards this might appear neglectful, but at the time it was normal practice for children of British parents living in India to be brought back for their education. There was a contemporary fear that, since in India the children would be mainly brought up by servants of Indian nationality, they could become too 'Indian' in their ways and outlook.

Rudyard was also receiving the type of education that was common at the time. He attended Hope House in Portsmouth, where the teaching was aimed at producing future Army and Navy officers – again, we might think this somewhat excessive considering he began there at six years old!

He enjoyed at least the company of the man of the house, who was known as 'Captain' Holloway although he had not risen above the rank of midshipman, and who took the boy on walks to see the ships at Portsmouth. However, as Kipling recalled in his autobiography, Mrs Holloway was generally unpleasant to him – perhaps, in her defence, he was still prone to tantrums. Be that as it may, things worsened after a few years when the 'Captain' died, leaving Rudyard to be bullied and beaten by Mrs Holloway and her son.

For a month each year, he got away from what he later called the 'House of Desolation' to stay with the family of his uncle, the artist Sir Edward Burne-Jones, in Fulham, London. On one such visit in early 1878, Sir Edward's wife Georgiana finally noticed that things were amiss with Rudyard. She saw that he was miserable and that his poor eyesight had not been looked into, and so she wrote to her sister Alice in India, who came back and took the children away to relatives. Soon after, Rudyard went to boarding school in Devon.

A rather worn image of Rudyard Kipling on a Southsea hoarding.

Lorne Lodge in Campbell Road.

We can get an impression of the type of ships that the 'Captain' took young Rudyard to see from HMS *Warrior*, which lies beside Portsmouth Historic Dockyard. It was built in 1860, and was the first iron-hulled armoured warship that could use steam power.

## H. G. Wells

H. G. Wells was older when he came to Portsmouth, verging on adulthood in the eyes of his contemporaries at least, and had a shorter stay. Herbert George Wells (1866–1946) was born in Bromley, Kent, the son of Joseph, the owner of a hardware shop who also played cricket professionally for Kent, and Sarah Wells. The family had financial problems that led to his mother living separately from his father while working as a housekeeper at Uppark, a country house some 4 miles south-east of Petersfield across the Sussex border.

Herbert had formed an early love of reading while in bed recovering from a broken leg. In 1880, around the time his mother went to Uppark, he was apprenticed to a draper in Windsor, then went back into education in Somerset and Sussex. His mother had decided that the best thing for the family (and its finances) was to get her sons out of school and into respectable apprenticeships. She had done the same for his two elder brothers, and in summer 1881, Herbert was again apprenticed as a draper at Hyde's Drapery Stores in Southsea.

Hyde's Drapers Stores was on the corner of King Street and Landport Street.

He went with trepidation to long hours and living above the store with other apprentices. In later life he admitted that, unlike the others, he found it difficult to put in the long periods of concentration necessary for particular tasks and to show due respect for his superiors. As a result, he was unhappy and recalled later that he was always being shouted at.

His only escapes were visited to his mother on rare holidays and when ill. In August 1883, though, he decided that he had had enough of the drudgery and gave up his apprenticeship, walking the 17 miles back to Uppark to explain himself to his undoubtedly very disappointed mother.

At the time, this must have been a soul-destroying experience for the lad, but he recovered by going into teaching and then developing a glittering literary

Uppark House is about 15 miles north-east of Portsmouth as the crow flies, and probably a fair few more as the dejected former apprentice trudges. Here it is seen from Telegraph Hill, a little over a mile to the south. The main house, which was built in the late seventeenth century, is in the middle. It is flanked by two buildings with identical frontages – the one on the left is the stables, while today the one on the right houses the restaurant. Uppark House and its grounds are now in the care of the National Trust.

career. His writings covered many subjects, and he used his experiences as a Portsmouth apprentice in his novels *Kipps: The Story of a Simple Soul* and *The Wheels of Chance*. Today, however, he is remembered chiefly as one of the pioneers of science fiction. Works such as *The War of the Worlds* and *The Time Machine* are still read and dramatised today, and Orson Welles' 1938 radio adaptation of the former famously frightened many Americans into believing that a Martian invasion of Earth was actually happening.

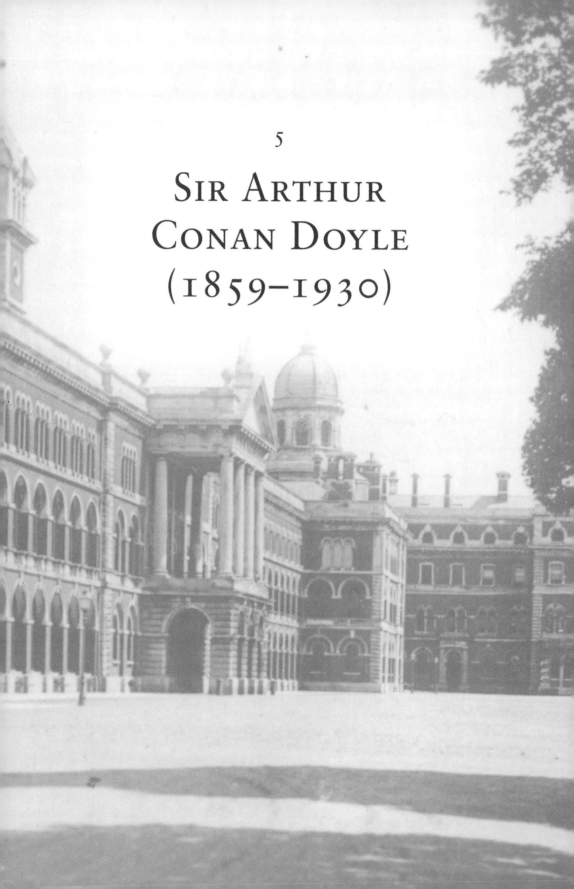

5

# SIR ARTHUR
# CONAN DOYLE
# (1859–1930)

The creator of Sherlock Holmes and writer of many adventure stories (1859–1930) was born in Edinburgh, and soon after was christened as Arthur Ignatius Conan Doyle. It seems that 'Conan' was one of his Christian names and his surname simply 'Doyle', but he is generally referred to as 'Conan Doyle' as though he had a double-barrelled surname, and sometimes followed this usage himself.

He qualified in medicine at Edinburgh University and then went travelling. His adventures included spending time as a ship's doctor on an Arctic whaling vessel, and he was already dabbling in writing, which led to him having stories published in magazines.

At a loose end, he was invited to join the successful (but rather questionable practice) of his former fellow Edinburgh student George Budd in Plymouth. This involved free consultations for patients, but with a liberal prescription of medicines, which were not free! Budd may have got away with this because Plymouth was a naval town with a large and often transient population that generally did not stay around long enough to ask too many questions. Conan Doyle joined him in May 1882. They quickly fell out, and so the following month saw Conan Doyle taking ship to another naval town, Portsmouth, where he thought he could try out Budd's method on his own.

Clarence Pier and Beach, Southsea.

*This and next page:* Clarence Pier, where Conan Doyle arrived in Portsmouth. The pier we see in the old image (taken around 1900) was built in 1861 and the pavilion was added in 1882. The pier was eventually destroyed in a German air raid in 1941.

Conan Doyle landed at Clarence Pier on Saturday 24 June, and was apparently struck by the sight of people parading nearby on Southsea Common. Ever enterprising, he bought himself a map of Portsmouth and soon worked out a good location for his practice, at No. 1 Bush Villas. This lay between the Southsea homes of many well-off people, and the more central shops that were their businesses. It was also between the Elm Grove Pentecostal church and a pub, The Bush Hotel, putting it in a locale that was easy to find and regularly frequented for other reasons!

On Saturday 1 July, Conan Doyle advertised his services in the *Portsmouth Evening News*. He was soon advised, though, that his method of free consultations would not work on the well-to-do locals. He was not immediately successful, which allowed him plenty of time for reading, writing more short stories for magazines as well as factual articles especially on medical subjects, and to develop his interest in spiritualism and the paranormal. During this time, his younger brother Innes came to stay and he, like Kipling, later attended Hope House.

Contrasting views of Southsea Common. The old picture was taken about twenty years after Conan Doyle's arrival here in 1882, and though fashions had changed in the intervening period, it gives a good idea of the sight that impressed him.

The site of Conan Doyle's surgery at No.1 Bush Villas in Elm Grove. That building was renamed 'Doyle House' by 1911.

He began to build his social life as well. In November 1883, he joined the Portsmouth Literary and Scientific Society, and gave his first talk, on his Arctic adventures on the whaler, the following month. During the previous summer he played several games for Portsmouth cricket club and also joined the local bowls club. In the autumn of the following year he attended a meeting at the Blue Anchor Pub in the Kingston Cross area, and became a founder member of the new Portsmouth Football Association Club. He played goalkeeper and sometimes full-back under the pseudonym A. C. Smith. This club disbanded in 1896, two years before the present club was formed.

In March 1885, he took into his own home the twenty-five-year-old Jack Hawkins, who had cerebral meningitis and soon died despite Conan Doyle's care. He also looked after Jack's mother and his sister, Louise, who was twenty-seven. Perhaps unsurprisingly, he fell for Louise and married her in Yorkshire in August of the same year.

In January 1887, Arthur and Louise began going to seances together, and at the same time he joined the Freemasons, being initiated into the Phoenix Lodge No. 257 at 110 High Street in Portsmouth. He was proposed by W. D. King, a former mayor of Portsmouth, and John Brickwood, described as 'one of the most influential brewers in the country', which indicates what an influential group he had become involved with.

The location of the Phoenix Lodge, No. 257 at 110 High Street.

In 1887 he began work on *Micah Clarke*, the story of a Puritan young man from Hampshire who joins the Monmouth Rebellion of 1685 against the Catholic King James II. This lengthy novel required shortening and other revisions before it was finally published in February 1889. The same year also saw the publication of the first of Conan Doyle's Sherlock Holmes novels, but I will leave that important matter until a little later.

The following year saw Conan Doyle interacting with other subjects of this book. On 20 November 1888, he gave a lecture to Portsmouth Literary and Scientific Society on George Meredith, who he admired. The next day he went to see his publisher in London, and at the Savile Club sat on the same table as Walter Besant, who had also written a novel about the Monmouth Rebellion, entitled *For Faith and Freedom*.

Arthur and Louise's first child, a daughter named Mary Louise, was born on 28 January 1889. After earlier consideration of the matter, in November 1890 Conan Doyle finally decided to leave Portsmouth for London, and did so in December.

Now to look at Sherlock Holmes. Conan Doyle wrote the first two novels featuring the great detective while living in Portsmouth – *A Study in Scarlet* and *The Sign of Four* – although he did not start out with the intention of writing a series, just one story.

His previous fiction had tended towards the fantastical, so *A Study in Scarlet* was a distinct departure. He wanted to take advantage of scientific advances, especially in crime detection, and came up with the idea of the human reasoning machine Sherlock Holmes as the way to portray how science was helping to fight crime in the modern world. The model for Holmes was Dr Bell, one of Conan Doyle's lecturers at Edinburgh University.

Holmes' assistant was Dr John Watson, who, as well as being the more 'human' intermediary who explains Holmes to the reader, had some interesting local links to the Portsmouth area. Firstly his name, which Conan Doyle probably adapted from another GP who was also a friend, Dr James Watson, whose practice was in Grove Road, just around the corner from Conan Doyle's own surgery. Like many of Conan Doyle's friends, he had served abroad in the armed forces. In giving his own story in *A Study in Scarlet*, Watson states that he undertook some of his training as a military doctor at 'Netley'. Netley is about ten miles west of Portsmouth on the Solent, and Watson undoubtedly means the Royal Victoria Hospital, which was a major military training establishment at the time. Conan Doyle seems to be thinking very locally here, for a reader from the Portsmouth area would probably know where he meant, but I doubt someone in northern England would. Watson then serves in India and is invalided out of the Army when wounded, and he specifically mentions returning to England at Portsmouth. Twice in later Holmes stories, Watson, while in London, yearns for 'the shingle of Southsea'.

*A Study in Scarlet* was published in 1887. It has a few oddities to those of us who have seen Holmes and Watson portrayed many times on television and

Grove Road, where the real Dr James Watson had his surgery.

A view of part of the Royal Victoria Hospital at Netley, taken around 1910. The hospital was built in the 1850s. The hospital complex was largely demolished in 1966, and the site is now in the Royal Victoria Country Park.

The Norrish Central Library in Guildhall Square houses the Richard Lancelyn Green Collection of memorabilia associated with Conan Doyle and Sherlock Holmes. This collection of items and documents was bequeathed by Richard Lancelyn Green in 2004 and can be viewed by appointment.

in film over the years. In the middle of the case, the normally intense Holmes takes a break to go to a concert, for instance. Also, the novel is broken into two parts – one covering the case in London, then an earlier story set in the American West that is meant to explain the London case. The two read rather oddly together, though, and it would be unduly generous to Conan Doyle to say that the slanderous portrayal of the Mormons in the second half is due to poor research.

Portsmouth City Museum in Museum Road has housed exhibitions connected with Conan Doyle and Sherlock Holmes. The building was constructed in 1893 as a military barracks, only becoming a museum in 1973.

This work was to be a one-off, but in 1889 an American publisher offered Conan Doyle £100 for a story, and he decided to bring back Holmes and Watson. *The Sign of Four* was published the following year, and tells a story linked to the British Raj in India. Conan Doyle had not been to India, but he had plenty of ex-military friends in Southsea to help with details. In the novel, the characters of Holmes and Watson are more established, and much closer to those portrayed by Basil Rathbone and Nigel Bruce and their successors.

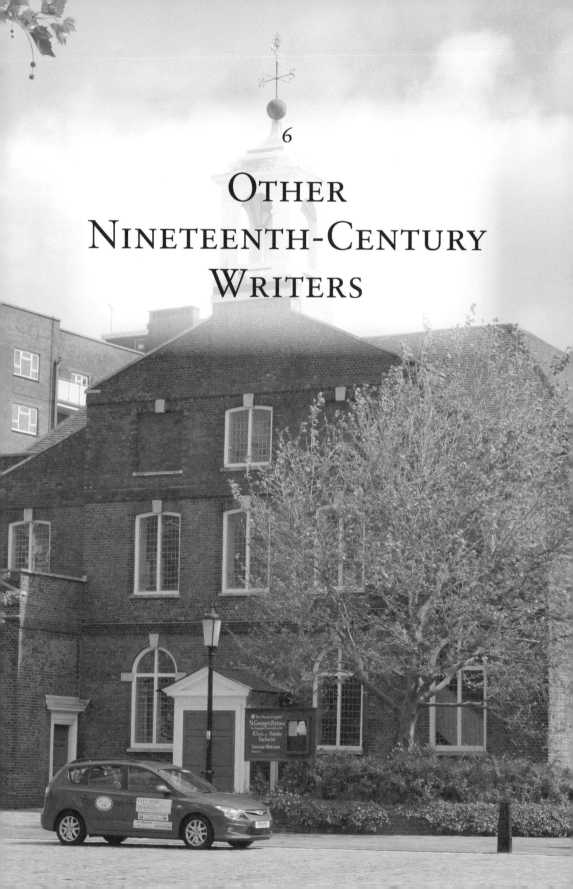

6

# OTHER
# NINETEENTH-CENTURY
# WRITERS

## Ivan Goncharov (1812–91)

At the end of the little peninsula known as Point or Spice Island, there is a very pleasant open area with seating, from which there are fine views of Portsmouth Harbour as well as the Spinnaker Tower and Gunwharf Quays. On the low wall that encloses this area there is a plaque that was unveiled by the Mayor of Portsmouth and the Russian ambassador to this country in 2012. This commemorated the 200th anniversary of the birth of the Russian writer, Ivan Goncharov. The location of the plaque is explained by a visit that Goncharov made here on the Russian frigate *Pallas* in 1852.

Goncharov's most famous work was *Oblomov*, the tale of a character who stayed in bed dreaming of great things, while never actually doing them. The story was much loved in the early days of the Communist state in Russia, since it was seen as an object lesson in how not to behave.

In memory of the great Russian writer
IVAN GONCHAROV
(1812, Simbirsk - 1891, St. Petersburg)
who stayed in Portsmouth in 1852
Памяти великого русского писателя
ИВАНА АЛЕКСАНДРОВИЧА ГОНЧАРОВА
(1812, Симбирск - 1891, Санкт - Петербург),
посетившего Портсмут в 1852 г.
Gift of the Government of the Ulyanovsk Region
Дар Правительства Ульяновской области

The plaque commemorating Ivan Goncharov and his visit to Portsmouth, written in both English and Russian.

The view from Spice Island by the Goncharov plaque.

George Meredith (1828-1909)

George Meredith was born in Portsmouth High Street, specifically at No. 74, near the harbour end of the street. His father and grandfather were naval outfitters. At the age of fourteen he was sent away to school in Germany, and became a novelist and poet in later life. Perhaps his best claim to fame from a modern perspective, however, was that he advised the young Thomas Hardy against having his first novel, *The Poor Man and the Lady*, published and to try writing something else. The novel was a satire on the rich, and Meredith felt that the resulting carpeting from critics would prevent Hardy from ever being published again.

George Meredith's birthplace. The houses have been rebuilt, and one named after him now has a different number. No. 73 in the middle of the block of five is 'Meredith House', while No. 74 is to the right as you look at them.

St George's church, Portsea.

The west front of Great Salterns, partly obscured by renovation work when this picture was taken. The house was built around 1820.

### Sir Walter Besant (1836–1901)

Sir Walter was a novelist and historian, and at one time a professor of mathematics. He was born in St George's Square, in a house that I believe no longer exists. He moved away at an early age, but in his autobiography he recalled the square as 'containing a curious sprawling barn of a church belonging to the time of George II'. This must be St George's church, which was built in the 1750s in New England Colonial style, and now advertises itself as 'The Shipwrights Church'.

The south side of Great Salterns, seen from the sea wall of Langstone Harbour.

## Sarah Doudney (1841-1926)

Sarah Doudney was born in Portsea and, like many others, was baptised at St Mary's church in Kingston. She wrote about fifty novels in all, one of which is of particular interest here. It was written in 1875 and entitled *The Great Salterns*. The novel was set in Portsmouth and the title referred to a real great house in an isolated location beside Langstone Harbour. Today, the location is less isolated, but the house still survives, having been converted into a pub and restaurant.

7

# NEVIL SHUTE
# (1899–1960)

Arguably the most important twentieth-century writer with Portsmouth connections was Nevil Shute (1899–1960). He was one of the world's bestselling novelists in the 1950s and 1960s and his novels continue to be popular today. *A Town Called Alice* is probably the best known of his works. His stories were often linked by themes of breaking down social barriers, although even a quick perusal of the synopses of his works tells you that many were adventures whose hero was a pilot. This reflects his own background as an aeronautical engineer, and while his own life did not quite match that of some of his heroes, it was eventful and his experiences before coming to Portsmouth tell a lot about the man.

Nevil Shute Norway, to give him his full name, was born in Ealing. His father was Secretary to the Post Office in Ireland for a while, including at the time of the Easter Rising of 1916, while his elder brother, Fred, joined the Army during the First World War and was killed in France in 1915. Nevil served in the Army himself at the end of that conflict, although he did not see combat.

When demobbed at the end of the war, Shute went to Balliol College, Oxford, to study engineering. During one vacation he did some unpaid work at the Aircraft Manufacturing Company (shortened to Airco) in Hendon – his first experience of aviation. Two of Airco's employees, C. C. Walker and Geoffrey de Havilland, were in the process of setting up their own de Havilland Aircraft Company while at Airco, and Shute took his voluntary help to them.

Shute graduated in 1922, and after a false start became a paid employee of de Havilland early the next year. He must have felt part of a great adventure – working for a new company on the cutting edge of the new technology of aeroplane design and construction, where the test pilots included de Havilland himself and great aviation pioneer Alan Cobham. Shute himself learned to fly in spring 1923. He was also beginning to write seriously, and perhaps the one downside to his life was that he had novels rejected by publishers in 1923 and 1924, although in later life he did admit that they were rather bad!

The ambitious Shute soon concluded that there were few opportunities for advancement at de Havilland, but realised that the burgeoning aviation industry was crying out for people, even with his relatively limited experience. In 1924, he went up to Yorkshire to work for Vickers Ltd on the development of the R100 airship.

The British government had seen airships as the best way to develop long-distance air travel, particularly with the various lands of the British Empire and Commonwealth. It decided to fund two projects, the private work on the R100 by Vickers, and the development of the R101 by an Air Ministry team based at Cardington in Bedfordshire – wags of the time called them the 'Capitalist' and the 'Socialist' airships. Shute's boss at Vickers was Barnes Wallis, now better remembered as the inventor of the 'bouncing bomb' of Dambusters fame. His job was 'Chief Calculator', working on such matters as calculating the stresses on various elements of the vessel.

While working on this project, Shute's first two novels were published: *Marazan* in 1926 and *So Disdained* three years later. He thought that Vickers would not take kindly to one of its most important employees spending time writing novels, even his spare time, so he just used his Christian names as his pen name to hide his identity.

Also in 1929, the R100 flew for the first time. Shute was on board during much of the testing, including a flight to Canada. The following year, the Air Ministry's R101 also flew, but crashed soon after at Beauvais in France on a flight to India, killing forty-eight of the fifty-four people on board, including the Government Minister, Lord Thomson, who initiated the airship programme.

In his autobiography, Shute is scathing about the system that had two airship types developed in competition with very little discussion and comparison between the two teams, and also about the pressures put on those involved in the government's R101 project in particular. However, he later admitted that his criticisms were too severe and others certainly did not share all his views, although it was accepted that the R101 team had been rushed into making the flight to India.

Be that as it may, Britain abandoned airships as being too dangerous, and aeroplanes were seen now as the air transport of the future. The now unemployed Shute therefore set up his own aircraft manufacturing company called Airspeed UK with a former colleague, Hessell Tiltman, and others from Vickers became their employees.

This was not a good time to start a business – the Great Depression occasioned by the Stock Market Crash of 1929 was beginning to bite, and much of Shute's energy was put into securing finance for the new company. After *Lonely Road* was published in 1931, Shute had to give up writing for five years.

Airspeed UK was originally based in York, close to where the Vickers airship team had been based, but the company needed a location with its own airfield. Sir Alan Cobham was on the company's board, and he was also beginning work in Hampshire on inflight refuelling, which led Shute to think about the South Coast.

He was attracted to Portsmouth, where the local corporation had built a new municipal aerodrome on what were then the outskirts of the city. It was close to Langstone Harbour, which as a broad and relatively calm stretch of water was seen as an ideal location from which to fly seaplanes, which were seen as having great potential at the time. Additionally, the location on the South Coast encouraged a contemporary idea that Langstone Harbour should be the terminal for flying boat services 'throughout the Commonwealth'.

Two views of the broad and tidal expanse of Langstone Harbour. The viewpoint of the photograph above is Ferry Road, Southsea, near the south-west 'corner' of the harbour. The one below was taken from the Farlington Marshes car park at the north-west 'corner'.

The industrial estates that now occupy the site of Portsmouth airport are in the centre in this view from Portsdown Hill.

Accordingly, Norway and Lord Grimthorpe (the chairman who had put much money into the company) visited Portsmouth in July 1932 and met the mayor at the Guildhall. The company subsequently moved to Portsmouth in March 1933, into a new factory at the aerodrome, which was rented from Portsmouth Corporation. They found northerners and midlanders who had come down to work for a summer happy to stay into the autumn because of the local climate and surroundings, and in 1934 the company became Airspeed Ltd after a public issue of shares, while the factory was extended several times over the next few years.

In 1936, *Lonely Road* was made into a film by Ealing Studios, and around this time Norway began writing again as the company built up and strengthened. *Ruined City* was his first novel of this period. In March 1937, an Airspeed Envoy was ordered for the King's Flight. Norway saw having one of his company's works in royal use as the high point of his aviation career and by

*Above and next page:* Views of Portsmouth Guildhall. The older picture was taken around 1925, so about seven years before Shute came to see the mayor. The original building, which dated from the 1880s, was heavily damaged during the Second World War and was rebuilt in the 1950s.

his own admission he began to lose interest in Airspeed afterwards. There were arguments at the company and the board removed him in April 1938.

The company was finally amalgamated with de Havilland in 1951, but its later history became of less concern to Norway, who was now making a comfortable living from book royalties and films. While at Airspeed, his holidays with his wife and two daughters were limited to weekends cruising on the Solent in their 10-ton boat *Skerdmore*, and they decided that now was the time to enjoy some foreign travel, an activity curtailed by the Second World War.

A building dating from Shute's time, beside what is still called Airport Service Road.

When war broke out, the family felt that their home near the Southsea seafront was too vulnerable to enemy attack, and moved first to two properties in Langstone where they stayed for relatively short times, then in 1941 to Pond Head House at South Hayling on Hayling Island. Shute soon became involved in design work for the military and spent much of the war as an officer in the Royal Navy. Some of the work was on aeroplanes, but he was also involved in designing a variety of often weird and wonderful equipment, from a gliding torpedo to a mobile flamethrower.

He continued his writing career during and after the war, when he began to get disillusioned with the state of this country. Following an earlier visit there, in 1950 he decided to emigrate to Australia, and it is in that country that his later works are generally set.

Road names on the industrial estate that commemorate Shute and his work. I wonder how many people now recognise the origin of these names. They probably know of 'Nevil Shute', but perhaps think that 'Marazan' is named from a place in Cornwall, and that 'Norway Lane' simply commemorates a connection with that country.

Shute's home at No.14 Helena Road, Southsea, is in the centre of this view. The house next door on the right has a blue plaque recording that Edwin Unwin, 'Hero of Gallipoli', resided there.

# 8

# Other Twentieth-Century Writers

The Tower House, as seen from the Round Tower.

William Lionel Wyllie (1851–1931)
The life of Wyllie overlapped a great deal with the previous century, but I will include him in this chapter because he made a particular contribution to the city in the twentieth century. Wyllie is deservedly known as a talented and prolific artist of maritime themes, but he also wrote books and illustrated them. His home while in Portsmouth was the distinctive Tower House on the harbour front, and named after the nearby Round Tower, a distinctive part of Portsmouth's defences.

In 1930 he completed a 42-foot-long panorama of the Battle of Trafalgar, which is still on display at the National Museum of the Royal Navy within Portsmouth Historic Dockyard.

The Round Tower is the only survivor of a pair built in the fifteenth century to guard a boom across the mouth of Portsmouth Harbour.

The National Museum of the Royal Navy.

Percy Westerman's home in Campbell Road.

Percy Westerman (1876–1959)

Percy Francis Westerman was born in New Road in Portsmouth's northern suburbs. In 1880, his family moved to a house in Campbell Road, Southsea. The house is almost at the opposite end of the street from Lorne Lodge, where the young Rudyard Kipling had lived a few years before. Westerman lived there for the next twenty years, a fact commemorated by a blue plaque that was unveiled on the house on 22 February 2013.

Like many local boys, Westerman attended Portsmouth Grammar School, then got a job in the dockyard. He began writing children's adventure books, mainly aimed at boys, with such success that in 1912 he was able to give up his day job and go to live on a houseboat in Dorset. In the end, he wrote 174 adventure books, and was this country's most popular writer in this genre of the 1930s.

The view along Campbell Road from the vicinity of Westerman's home, in the direction of Lorne Lodge.

The Sea Scout Headquarters, located between the Round Tower and Point. Westerman was a strong supporter of the local sea scouts, and wrote a special story for them.

The site of Richard Aldington's birth, now occupied by a more recent building.

Richard Aldington (1892-1962)

Richard Aldington was born at No. 50 High Street, opposite what is now Portsmouth Cathedral. He was wounded on the Western Front during the First World War, and it has been suggested that his experiences of the war left him with Post-Traumatic Stress Disorder, a condition unrecognised by the medical profession at the time.

He went on to write poetry, novels and factual works. Aldington was one of the sixteen best British poets of the First World War, whose names were set on a memorial in Poets' Corner, Westminster Abbey. The best known of his novels was *Death of A Hero*, published in 1929, in which the main character becomes

rtsmouth,
r Memorial.

*This and next page:* The War Memorial was originally erected to commemorate the dead of the First World War. It lies between Guildhall Square and Victoria Park. The old view was probably taken in the 1920s. Today, as my photograph shows, the outlying machine gunners (one of whom fights on despite a head wound) have been moved back to leave an open space in front. On the right of that shot, there is the separate memorial to the dead of the Second World War.

disillusioned while serving in the war and loses the ability to relate to his wife and friends, mirroring some of Aldington's own experiences.

In 1955, his biography of Lawrence of Arabia was published. This was seen as a virulent attack on a national hero, and though it revealed new details of Lawrence's life, it also made accusations that are now not generally accepted. The episode has affected both Lawrence's and Aldington's reputations ever since.

James Clavell (1924–94)

James Clavell (to use his pen name) is unique among the subjects of this book in coming to Portsmouth solely for his education. He was born in Australia while his father, a Royal Navy officer, was seconded to the Australian Navy, and must have been posted to Portsmouth afterwards, for his son was educated at Portsmouth Grammar School.

Following his education, James joined the Royal Artillery and suffered a great deal as a prisoner-of-war of the Japanese. Several years after the war ended, he

Although founded in 1732, Portsmouth Grammar School only moved to its present site at the landward end of the High Street in 1926. The building into which it moved had been the Cambridge Barracks, and was constructed in the 1850s.

emigrated to the United States and became a successful writer. Perhaps his two most famous works are *King Rat*, based on his experiences under the Japanese, and *Shogun*, the story of an Englishman in Japan some 400 years ago that was made into a very successful television series starring Richard Chamberlain.

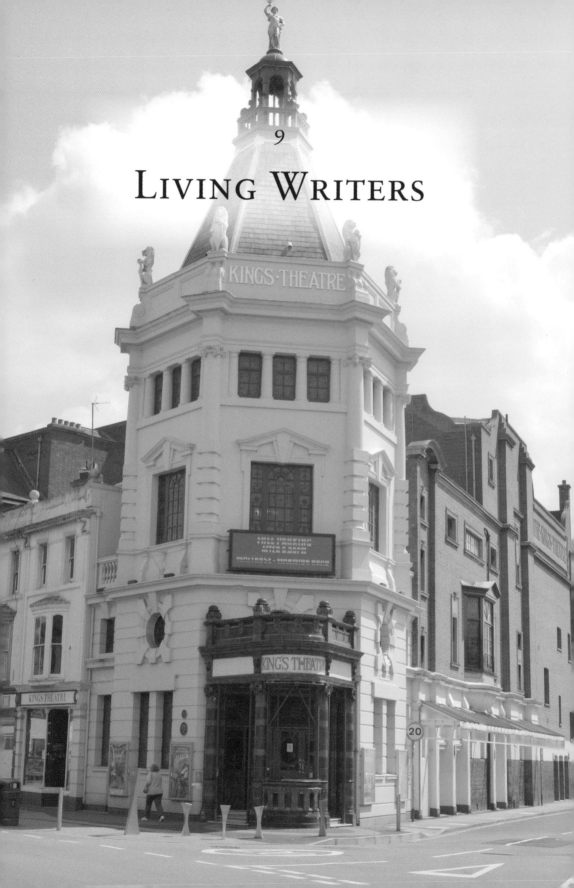

9

# LIVING WRITERS

This final chapter is a look at some of the authors who are continuing the strong tradition of Portsmouth literature today.

The King's Theatre, Southsea, where Michelle Magorian trained as a child.

*Literary Portsmouth*

St. Thomas Road, Gosport.

Views of St Thomas Road, the old one probably dating from the 1920s. It is a typical Gosport terraced street, of the type on which 'April Grove' is based.

Kingstone Crescent Police Station, where a little girl goes to report that her father is missing in the opening chapter of *Turnstone*.

Michelle Magorian
Michelle Magorian was born in Portsmouth, and like so many people in the city her father was in the Navy. Her most famous work is the children's story *Goodnight Mister Tom*, first published in 1981, which tells the story of a boy who is evacuated from London to the countryside during the Second World War, where he meets an old recluse, Tom Oakley. The story was made into a film in the 1990s, with John Thaw playing the title role. Michelle is an actress as well as a writer and still lives in Portsmouth.

The father in *Turnstone* has been living in a flat within a converted former hotel near South Parade Pier and Southsea Common, similar to those seen in the picture.

An evening view of Port Solent. Much of the action in *Turnstone* takes place around this newly constructed leisure and residential centre near the top of Langstone Harbour.

Farlington Marshes, the RSPB nature reserve where Faraday spends much of his leisure time.

Faraday's home is described as being on Portsmouth's Langstone Harbour waterfront and visible from Farlington Marshes. There may be some poetic licence in this, but the Longshore Way area just about fits the bill.

*Above and below*: In *The Take*, the Gunwharf Quays development (under construction at the time of the novel's writing) is the centre of much of the story. Here are two views of the development's harbour frontage, one including the Spinnaker Tower (*below*).

Lilian Harry

Across the harbour now to Gosport, where Lilian Harry was born and lived through the Second World War as a young child. Her home was in one of the streets of terraced houses built as Gosport extended inland from Portsmouth Harbour. Lilian's April Grove series of novels reflects this experience, being set in the fictitious Gosport street of that name during the war years, although plenty of real locations in the Portsmouth area are mentioned.

Graham Hurley

Continuing the theme of novels set in the local area, over the past decade and a half or so Graham Hurley has written a series centred around his Detective Inspector Joe Faraday. Faraday is a keen birdwatcher who does not like taking orders and, as is essential for such novels, he has various ups-and-downs in his family life and relationships. One of the team of detectives who work for him is Paul Winter, an even worse rebel than Faraday, who does not do things by the book if he can help it.

I have chosen here some locations from the first two novels of the series, *Turnstone* and *The Take*, to illustrate the local setting.

Also in *The Take*, we are introduced to Winter's home life when his wife is diagnosed with cancer. They live in a bungalow in Bedhampton, examples of which are depicted here.

# Bibliography

Ackroyd, Peter, *Dickens* (Sinclair-Stevenson Limited, London, 1990)

Austen, Jane, *Mansfield Park* (1814; Headline Review, 2006)

Barker, Juliet, *Agincourt* (Little, Brown, London, 2005)

Brome, Vincent, *H. G. Wells – A Biography* (Longmans, Green and Co., London, 1951)

Conan Doyle, Sir Arthur, *A Study in Scarlet* (1887; Pocket Penguin Classics, 2007)

Conan Doyle, Sir Arthur, *The Sign of Four* (1890; Pocket Penguin Classics, 2010)

Dickens, Charles, *Nicholas Nickleby* (1839; Penguin Classics, 1978)

Foot, Michael, *The History of Mr Wells* (Doubleday, London, 2005)

Gilmour, David, *The Long Recessional – The Imperial Life of Rudyard Kipling* (John Murray, London, 2002)

Hurley, Graham, *The Take* (Orion, London, 2000)

Hurley, Graham, *Turnstone* (Orion, London, 2001)

Jennings, Charles, *A Brief Guide to Jane Austen: The Life and Times of the World's Favourite Author* (Running Press/Robinsons, 2012)

Lycett, Andrew, *Conan Doyle – The Man Who Created Sherlock Holmes* (Weidenfeld & Nicolson, London, 2007)

Sadden, John, *The Portsmouth Book of Days* (The History Press, Stroud, 2011)

Sadden, John, *Portsmouth – a Pocket Miscellany* (The History Press, Stroud, 2012)

Shute, Nevil, *Slide Rule – The Autobiography of an Engineer* (1954; Vintage, 2009)